Monkeys & Apes

Beverley Randell

Contents

Monkeys have tails

There are many
kinds of monkeys,
and they
all have tails.

Some monkeys
can hang
by their tails.

Most monkeys
live in trees
and eat fruit
and leaves.
Other monkeys
look for food
on the ground.

Apes don't have tails

This is not a monkey,
because it does not have a tail.
It is a small ape, called a **gibbon**.
Gibbons swing by their hands
and jump from tree to tree
in the **tropical rainforest**.

Do apes have tails?

Some monkeys from South America

Because monkeys have small noses, they can't smell very well. But they have good ears, and they hear well. Some monkeys call loudly to let other monkeys know where they are.

No. Apes do not have tails.

Most animals can't see colours, but monkeys and apes can. They can see when flowers and fruit are ready to eat. They can see small insects moving.

When monkeys jump from branch to branch, they **need** to see well.

Can monkeys see colours?

Some monkeys from Asia

Not long ago,
one of these
Asian monkeys
started to wash
some of its food
in the sea.

Soon
other monkeys
copied it.
Monkeys learn
from each other.

Yes. Monkeys can see colours.

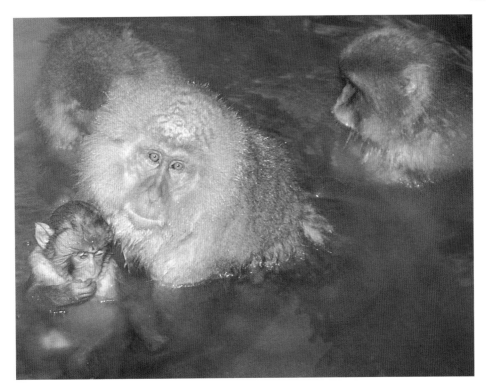

These Asian monkeys live
in a cold place.
They have very thick fur.
They have learned
to sit in hot pools
to keep warm in the winter.

Do all monkeys live
in the tropical rainforest?

Baboons live in Africa

Young **baboons** ride
on their mothers' backs.
Monkeys' feet are like hands,
and little baboons
have four hands
for hanging on with.

No. Some monkeys live in cold places.

Baboons live together
in big **troops**.
They love to feed
on fallen fruit.

Most monkeys
and apes
take care of
each other's fur.
This is called
grooming.

Where do baboons live?

Gorillas live in Africa

Gorillas are the biggest
and the heaviest of all the apes.
They eat leaves, and they live
in the tropical rainforest.
Gorillas are gentle, and they
live together in small troops.

Baboons live in Africa.

Gorillas sleep on the ground
in nests made of leaves.
Each gorilla makes a new nest
every night.

Babies sleep with their mothers,
and they drink their mothers' milk.

Do gorillas live by themselves?

Wild chimpanzees live in Africa

Chimpanzees are smaller than gorillas. They live in the tropical rainforest, too. They make  their sleeping nests up in the trees, using branches and leaves.

Chimpanzees eat fruit, flowers, seeds, nuts, green leaves and insects, and sometimes they catch and eat small animals.

No. Gorillas live together in small troops.

How chimpanzees catch termites

Chimpanzees have learned to push long thin sticks into **termites'** nests.

When the stick is pulled out, it will have some termites hanging on to it.

Chimpanzees like eating termites.

Where do wild chimpanzees live?

Chimpanzees are like us

Young chimpanzees love to climb.
They often play with each other,
but if something scares them
they run back to their mothers.

Chimpanzees pat and hug
each other, and sometimes
they hold hands just as we do.
Their fingers and their thumbs
are like ours.
Families stay near each other
all their lives.

Chimpanzees are like us,
in many ways.

Chimpanzees live in Africa,
in the tropical rainforest.

Do chimpanzees have thumbs?

Where monkeys and apes live

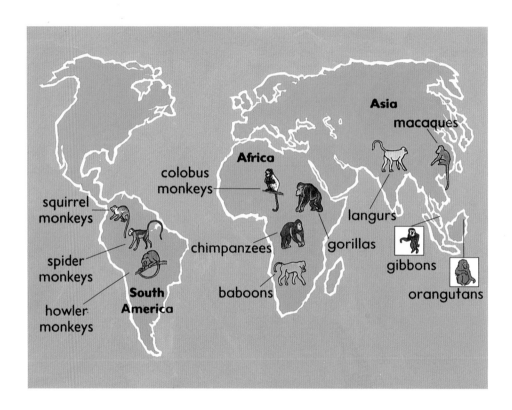

Yes. Chimpanzees have thumbs.